THE HISTORY
OF THE
COLONY CLUB

1903–1984

by

Anne F. Cox

IN RECOGNITION

The president and Governors of the Colony Club are deeply grateful to Mrs. Howard E. Cox for the creation of this book.

With her charm, perseverance, love and dedication to the Club she has ensured a permanent record of its history and achievements, giving pleasure and inspiration to all our members.

Privately printed 1984
for the Colony Club, New York City.
Printed in the United States of America.

Contents

PICTURE CREDITS

Preface

THE HISTORY OF THE COLONY CLUB was born on the day
that Mrs. Edward T. Chase and Mrs. Philip D. Wiedel asked me to
do a fashion revue for the Seventy-Fifth Anniversary of the Club.
I immediately said yes, thinking it would take several friends and
myself about seven weeks. A few days later, however, I realized that
we had no clothes, no workroom, no lights, no runway, no closet
or storage space for costumes, and especially no simple system of
records for the seventy-five-year existence of the Club to help my
research. The project eventually involved several hundred members
with a dozen or so working up to sixteen months, and led to my
producing four lectures on the history of the Club and ultimately
to my writing this book.

This work could not have been accomplished without the help
and support of many members, particularly Mrs. William A.
Chisolm, who spent many hours with me photographing old newspapers, prints and photographs in our Archives; and especially Miss
Suzanne S. Frisbie who, with her expertise in the publishing world,
gave generously of her time and professionalism.

Mrs. Charles S. Whitman, Jr., assisted by Mrs. Howard F. Beir,
toiled tirelessly during the hot summer days compiling committee
lists and proofreading names. My thanks to each and every one but

especially to my patient and supportive husband, Howard E. Cox, who kept me always pointed toward the printer.

Finally, the history of the Colony Club would not be complete without including our managers. In late 1905, two years before the first clubhouse was completed, Mr. Frank L. Wheatland came as cashier. He became our manager for the next forty years. In 1945, he unionized the Club's employees under the direction of our President, Mrs. Henry James, and the Board of Governors. He died of a heart attack in 1946.

The next manager was with us only a few months. (Who could ever take the place of a manager who had devoted himself so completely to the Club for over forty years?.)

Then the Board of Governors decided to hire a management consultant company. For the next three and one half years, Blaikie, Miller and Hines managed the Club. Mr. Blaikie suggested we hire Mr. Henry Hewer of the Greenbrier Hotel as our manager. This was a good recommendation: Mr. Hewer remained with us for twenty-five years between March 1949 and April 1974, when he retired. We were then exceedingly lucky to have Mr. Harold C. Gibbons become our "new" manager: he has continued to maintain the Club's high standards. Mr. Peter Pagnutti has been our comptroller for the past twenty-six years, working with Mr. Hewer and Mr. Gibbons. He has kept our financial affairs in perfect order.

How fortunate we have been with them and all of our staff.

ANNE F. COX

EXCERPT FROM THE INAUGURAL SPEECH
OF THE COLONY CLUB'S FIRST PRESIDENT

In anticipation, the pleasure of this dinner was very much diminished after I was told the other day that I would have to make a speech, as the last thing I have ever pictured myself as being was "an after dinner speaker." Every other sensation now, however, pales before that of gratitude to all you kind people who, by your presence here tonight, show not only your interest in the Colony Club, but in what the Colony Club hopes to do.

Women's clubs have existed in New York before for a distinct cause: Daughters of the American Revolution, Civic League and many others; or for a distinct class: students, artists, etc. But there has been no inclusive woman's club before this with a purely social object, at least not on such a scale as this. Therefore it is best now to make some statement of the policy of this Club.

A remark a number of people have made is, "A woman's home should be her club." They are quite right in that her home should be her first interest, but the Club if used in the right way should enrich the home.

Here every Tuesday afternoon there will be an opportunity for consideration of something worthwhile.

In the first week of the month, a lecture on a literary topic by someone qualified to speak with the highest authority on his or her particular subject.

The following week a conference to discuss the various problems of the day in politics and social science.

On the third Tuesday we have planned to have loan exhibitions of laces, miniatures, book bindings, etc., and in the last week of each month, we hope to have music of the best sort, or talks on music.

Then there are the various means of encouraging regular exercise, which is one of the things most essential to health and so to happiness, and very hard to obtain during the winter months in New York.

Again in this great city of ours it is very difficult not to sacrifice the individual to a cause, for with the best intentions in the world it is almost impossible to see even one's best friends as often as one wishes to and should, unless they are working with us in some charitable or other enterprise or perhaps belong to the same bridge class. This tendency to lose the personal element from our lives is much to be regretted, and the Club as a common meeting ground for women of all interests should do much to obviate it. And so from this building where we sit tonight a woman should go to her home with a broadened point of view, and her life enriched by contact with the best in Art, Literature, Music and Civics, and the wish to extend her interest beyond just a small group or clique of people.

If this policy, so near all our hearts, is to be made effective, we need the help of every good woman to create influence, and of every man who is willing to take the Club seriously because he believes in the power of his wife or sister as women in this Community.

We believe that this Club can have a very real effect on American life because every city in this land turns to New York to set the pace and the pattern of its morals and manners.

According to the British Ambassador in his "American Commonwealth," women mean more in America than anywhere else in the world, and we believe that this Club can give definiteness to this thought.

—Florence J. Harriman
March 9, 1907

The Presidents

MRS. J. BORDEN HARRIMAN   1904–1917

A brilliant and forceful first president—with charm and humor (and never at a loss for words)—outstanding in everything she undertook. She presided while the first clubhouse was planned and built, and also was president when our present location was selected and the clubhouse built. How lucky we were to have her! After she resigned she was among the first to go to France and drive an ambulance at the front.

MISS RUTH MORGAN 1917–1924

Miss Ruth Morgan became our second president when Mrs. Harriman and Mrs. Irvin, president and vice-president for our first thirteen years, resigned together.

This was a progressive time for women. In 1920, the 19th Amendment was passed. Many members of the Colony Club had joined Mrs. O.H.P. Belmont's Political Equality Association, and felt that their efforts had at last "pushed it over the top."

The Governors, supported by President Morgan, voted that members "be allowed to use the swimming pool without wearing bathing suits." (This edict has since been rescinded as the pool is now coed!)

And Miss Morgan suggested that men's clubs have a "women's advisory committee to guide the men's clubs."

MRS. SEYMOUR L. CROMWELL   1924–1929

In 1925 the waiting list was over 1,000, and the president in the happy "twenties" reported that: "No one can doubt that as a group we are the most financially astute, the most intelligent and intellectual, the most beautiful and the most elegant."

MRS. JAMES A. BURDEN 1929–35

An astute and strong leader, she piloted the Club successfully through the dark Depression days—including paying off the mortgage in 1931, three years ahead of time.

MRS. MONTGOMERY HARE 1935-1941

*She had the ability to make everyone work together—"a charming little lady. . .
whom you wanted to put your arms around and help." Under her presidency, in
1939 the gymnasium was turned into a workroom to aid the war effort.*

MRS. HENRY JAMES 1941–1946

*Extremely efficient and with great business ability, she guided and ran the Club
successfully through all the desperate shortages of food and help during the war
years. Under her presidency the Club was unionized and the welfare committee
work was taken over by the union.*

MRS. LANGBOURNE M. WILLIAMS, JR.   1946–52

A brilliant president with a fabulous memory for every detail—charming and delightful to all. Under her presidency, the staff was put on a five-day week.

MRS. REGINALD P. ROSE   1952–1957

She was a leader with many talents, a judge for prominent flower shows—a great knowledge of antiques. She had the ability to accomplish things unobtrusively and subtly. She was president during the Fiftieth Anniversary Celebration in 1953. Mrs. Rose was also co-chairman of the Seventy-Fifth Anniversary Fashion Revue on December 7, 1978, which ended with her saying:

> *The Colony Club is the sum of countless people; members and staff who have worked together to make a wonderful whole. We salute those who had the vision and courage to make a start in such a new field as a woman's club. We count ourselves lucky to have worked with this courageous group of women.*

MRS. GORDON RENTSCHLER 1957–1962

Her deep concern and real interest in all the members of the Club made her years as president particularly effective. She channeled both young and old members into using their abilities for the benefit of the Club—and to social responsibilities.

MRS. HERMANN G. PLACE   1962–1966

The perfect president for the turbulent sixties. Innovative and supportive of the young and beloved by all ages; naturally efficient without effort. During the "blue-jean era" Mrs. Place was the first to wear a beautifully tailored pants suit to the Club for lunch.

Her daughter, Mrs. Cochran B. Supplee, is now (1984) the First Vice President.

MRS. WALTER S. GIFFORD 1966–1972

A calming influence during our Vietnam war years. She made a just and wise decision for every problem large or small. A true mediator. A former tennis champion, she was particularly interested in our Bath and Athletics Department.

MRS. ROBERT JAMES LEWIS   1972–1976

One of our most distinguished presidents. Truly a Grande Dame—with a Bryn Mawr degree and a surprising sense of fun and wit hidden under a dignified demeanor.

MRS. CHARLES I. PIERCE   1976–1980

Perfection in every sense—chic and charming. The ability to make friends—with no one envious. The calm and hard-working president during our Seventy-Fifth anniversary year.

MRS. STANLEY F. REED, JR.   1980–1984

One of our youngest presidents under whose able leadership the Club flourished with many new younger members joining and becoming active. Her dignity, wisdom and strength made her an admired executive and friend to all.

MRS. BRADLEY I. COLLINS   1984–

Her beauty, warmth and compassion, combined with keen intelligence, endear her to the membership.

One

THE FIRST CLUBHOUSE
1907–1915
or
The Teacup Revolution

W HEN REVOLUTION AND TEA are mentioned, we think of the Boston Tea Party and the beginning of our country's fight for independence.

For the women who founded the Colony Club more than eighty years ago, it was almost as revolutionary a beginning—for it heralded, in particular, the fight for equality and independence. These were able, patriotic women working together with great courage and intelligence toward a noble objective: that women should be involved in society outside the home and thereby help to make the world a better place to live in.

We take this involvement almost for granted now in 1984, but the America of eighty years ago was a very different world—a world in which women occupied only the fringes.

In 1901, President McKinley was assassinated, and Vice-President Roosevelt, "Teddy," became President. Ellis Island was crowded with immigrants. Child labor was commonplace. There were only a few automobiles on the streets, with hobbyists and Sunday drivers behind the wheel. Most people most of the time still depended on the horse. And airplanes had a long way to go before they were "up and away," though the first one had left the ground for a few seconds the year the Colony Club was formally organized in 1903.

The lifespan of the turn-of-the-century woman was forty-five years, and for most women those years would be spent at home. In the particular milieu in which the Club's founders lived, even for those who were exceptionally talented, the only career most women could look forward to was marriage—and even to marry they would need their parents' permission. After the marriage, their activities were almost completely limited by their husbands' interests.

Aside from shopping, about the only pleasure left was what one early Colonist, a Club founder, Miss Elizabeth Marbury, called "senseless visiting." This endless, reciprocal "calling" involved tea parties, virtually the only acceptable functions for women unaccompanied by their husbands, so that a lady's social life in the daytime consisted mainly of going to tea parties or giving them. Pouring tea and doing it with grace was an important aspect in her life. Teaching their daughters to pour tea properly was taken seriously by mothers, and indeed this social function was considered important enough to be included in the curriculum of proper schools for young ladies.

Ladies were banned from voting (politicians believed women might vote to stop child labor), from restaurants (if they were unescorted), from saloons (for obvious reasons), from tobacco shops (a woman was arrested in New York for smoking in the street) and from men's clubs.

So it became obvious that what these women needed, first of all, was a place of their own to gather, socialize, exercise, study and work. They needed a club. But what an uproar such an idea caused!

Ex-President Cleveland, for instance, thundered, "Women's clubs are harmful. The best and safest club is a woman's home. A life retired is well inspired." A great many clergymen agreed with him, preaching from the pulpit that women's clubs and women entering the working world would spell the end of the American home and family.

Nonetheless, in the year 1900, on Baileys Beach in Newport, a group of five women discussed forming a club in New York City that would have enough space for a lawn tennis court (that was the most important consideration) and comfortable rooms and accommodations for rest and relaxation. It was during this beachside conference that the Colony Club was born.

By the following year twenty women were seriously involved; each contributed $10 toward the "Women's Social and Athletic Club." The lawn tennis court posed the first real problem, for even in 1901 land in Manhattan was a scarce and costly commodity. The top of the Plaza Hotel, which was then in the process of being built, was briefly considered but dismissed as impractical, and although the roof of some newly built stables at 41st Street and Third Avenue was offered, the ladies felt that going there for tennis would mar the "social aspect" of their new club.

But soon the founders were thinking beyond lawn tennis. In 1903 forty women raised over $400,000 to buy land and build their own building from scratch. On January 20, a memorable day, 120 to 124 Madison Avenue at 30th Street was purchased. It was a location convenient to the homes of many of the Club's founders. This first step augered well, for while many men were saying that women lacked the business sense to establish and run a club of their own, it turned out that a few months later they could have sold their land at a $50,000 profit. Wisely, they refused, for they were founding a club, not speculating in real estate—but for the first time there must have been a few eyebrows raised at the Union Club. Ironically, the founders soon formed a men's "advisory committee," but it appears that from the very beginning the women were doing very well on their own.

The Club now had an address, but it still needed a name, and among those considered were the Bernard Club, the Liberty Club and the Town Club. Finally one was chosen: "Play Fair." I think our first name told a lot about our founders, and I like it. Three weeks later, however, it was discarded and "Colony" was chosen in its place. The new name is better than its predecessor; with

"Colony Club" the founders retained the sense that something new and daring was being undertaken. The members, of course, called themselves "Colonists," the name of many of their ancestors over a hundred and twenty-seven years before.

In 1904, Stanford White was chosen as the architect for the new clubhouse, which turned out to be his last work. After he was killed in 1906, in the climax of the greatest social scandal of the decade, his widow was made the Colony Club's second honorary member.

When Stanford White submitted his first plans the ladies thought them not extensive enough. In April they voted to accept his second plan, which included a "parking room" for members' dogs under eight pounds (whether heavier dogs were allowed inside or excluded entirely was not recorded in Club minutes). The design for the clubhouse was patterned on a house in South Carolina that Mr. White liked.

While studying the plans carefully, the women discovered that Mr. White had made no provision for getting food from the first-floor kitchen to the fifth-floor dining room. This was quickly rectified, however, and the effort to turn the blueprints into reality was begun.

With Mr. White's urging, the Club Governors prevailed on Elsie de Wolfe (herself one of the first members) to leave the stage and decorate the Colony Club in the same way she had done her own house. It was Miss de Wolfe's first professional decorating job. Her later successes included the interior of the Frick House, J.P. Morgan's opera box and Brooks Hall at Barnard College. She threw herself into this first project with great enthusiasm, traveling all over Europe in her search for special wallpaper and carpets and supervising every detail (including locks and keys made according to her own design).

She did, however, admit to a few moments of panic. One of the most acute of these must have been when the Governors approved only $25,000 of her proposed budget of $30,000. She surmounted this crisis and, it appears, all the others.

The first clubhouse at 120-124 Madison Avenue at 30th Street. The architect was Stanford White. It was to be his last building.

The Ballroom and Lounge in the first clubhouse.

(ABOVE) The Trellis Room in the first clubhouse. The decorator for the Club was Elsie DeWolfe. It was her first decorating job. (BELOW) The private Dining Room.

A good example of Miss de Wolfe's approach was the Trellis Room, which was pictured in many of the decorating magazines of the time. A typical description said the room "was painted a soft green, and the furniture was of wood and straw." In the lounge and other public rooms she used large patterned chintz. The linens she chose came from Paris, and a great deal of the furniture was from Baltimore. Partly as a result of her work on the Colony Club, Miss de Wolfe was known as "the Chintz Decorator." It was a title she loved.

As the official opening approached, a wide array of minor matters had to be attended to. Miss Elizabeth Marbury, the able head of the House Committee, unveiled the Club's coat of arms. It depicted a beaver, signifying activity, and a crown, suggesting that in democratic America each woman was a queen.

Blue and buff were chosen as the colors. They had been those of our Continental Army and were therefore considered perfect for this association of latter-day Colonists. The menservants' blue-and-buff uniforms were made in Paris for the average-sized man, and correspondingly average-sized men were hired to fit them.

The Colony Club was on its way, but it had not yet begun to gather members. How was it to attract the prominent women the founders wanted? They finally decided to write to women all over the United States whose names stood for achievement in art, literature, music and philanthropy. While 321 accepted the invitation to join, 800 refused. It was later learned that many women were urged by their husbands to send their regrets.

Here is a partial list of some of those early members:

• Maud Adams, of *Peter Pan* fame.

• Amy Lowell, poetess, critic and the first woman to have an article published in *The Atlantic Monthly*. (She also enjoyed smoking big black cigars.)

• Louise Lee Schuyler, great-granddaughter of Alexander Hamilton and the founder of the Bellevue School of Nursing. In 1908 she started the First Committee for Aftercare of the Insane.

• Elizabeth Marbury, the best-known literary agent and play-broker of her time. Her clients included George Bernard Shaw, Oscar Wilde, Jerome Kern and P.G. Wodehouse.

• Kate Douglas Wiggin, author of *Rebecca of Sunnybrook Farm*.

• Frances Hodgson Burnett, author of *Little Lord Fauntleroy*, *The Little Princess* and *Sara Crewe*.

• Carolyn Wells, author of *The Patty Books* (a series of children's stories) and an outstanding humorist of her day.

• Emily Price Post, the social arbiter.

• Jane Addams, founder of a famous neighborhood center in Chicago that set a pattern for social services in other cities.

As all these particulars were being ironed out—design, decorating and the membership drive—many men continued to laugh at the thought of a women's club succeeding. When (not if) it failed, they joked, "the Union Club [which was at 21st Street and Fifth Avenue] will take it over as an annex." It wasn't amusing to be laughed at. Still, through the crises of those early years, especially a strike that delayed construction of the clubhouse for some months, the Governors wondered whether they really could do it.

Miss de Wolfe and the Governors worked feverishly on last-minute details as the hoped-for date of the completion of the clubhouse, January 1907, approached. An English housekeeper was engaged. The entrance wallpaper, which was not thought handsome enough, was replaced. Finally, on March 9, 1907, the clubhouse was ready to welcome members. It was a new beginning all around. When Mrs. H. Fairfield Osborne asked what she should do with the old Club reports she had been keeping at home, she was told to burn them. What a shame! It would have been interesting to have those records in our archives. However, there would be paperwork enough now that the Club was open and operating; within a month the secretary asked for a desk, an assistant and, amazingly, a typewriter!

Contemporary newspaper descriptions of the clubhouse mention the beautiful ballroom and note that the swimming pool, with its lighting fixtures draped with artificial grapes and vines, was reminiscent of old Rome. The gymnasium, the finest in the country, had

Elsie DeWolfe said the following in The Delineator *magazine for November 1911:*

"Why did I leave the stage for the field of Interior Decorating? The Colony Club loomed. The governors were my intimate personal friends. They said: if you will leave the theatre you can have the Colony as your first commission. We want a woman to do the decorating of this women's club."

Amy Lowell was a famous writer and poet. In spite of a puritan demeanor, she enjoyed black cigars and smoked them in public. She called our restless afternoon lecture patrons "a wristwatch audience."

Anne Morgan, the Colony Club's first treasurer, was known for her war work in France in World War I. In the early 1900s she also applied for membership with the Shirtwaist Strikers Union.

a running track (the word "jogging" was not yet used) suspended by brackets from the ceiling. The track was forty-nine yards long. Thirty-six laps made a mile. The gymnasium equipment was based on a combination of Turkish, German, Swedish and French exercise methods. Members' gym suits consisted of wide bloomers and sailor blouses. They were dark blue with Colonial-buff trimmings. They also had chemisettes "like shields to protect the throat," according to one account. Women who came from out of town could use little booths called "prinkeries."

In her opening speech on March 9, 1907, Mrs. J. Borden Harriman, the Colony Club president, recalled with some satisfaction what President Cleveland had thundered about women's clubs. She went on, "From this building. . . a woman should go to her home . . .enriched by contact with the best in Art, Literature, Music and Civics. . . . This Club can have a very real effect on American life because every city in this land turns to New York to set the pace and the pattern of its morals and manners."

Mrs. Harriman led the Colony Club for its first thirteen years. She was a remarkable woman who, for her time, was very active politically. When Woodrow Wilson became President, he appointed her to the Capital and Labor Commission. In 1937, thirty years after she became our first president, President Roosevelt made her the first woman minister to a foreign country—Norway. Her full-length portrait, by Alexander, completed in 1909, now hangs in the second floor.

There were many anxious moments during those first months, frequently over cash flow. At one point the House Committee reported that it had lost $6,600, while the Bath Department made $1,500. But the Club was manifestly a success from the beginning. Some fifty-five women attended the first lecture, and $4,500 was soon appropriated by the Governors to enclose the roof garden. Elsie de Wolfe ordered two Dutch stoves from Paris to heat this new room. Meanwhile, the tearoom was turned into a talking area.

Previously, the public hall had been the only place members were allowed to sit and carry on a conversation.

By January 1907 the membership had risen from 472 to 697 resident members and from 20 to 110 non-resident members. About the same time the Governors took their first recorded punitive action. The ten- to sixteen-year-old junior members (whose dues were $10 per year) had evidently been behaving too rambunctiously in the gym. The Governors, asserting that the clubhouse had been "imposed on and ill used by them," eliminated the junior-member category. The Bath and Athletic Department flourished even without the youngsters, holding popular classes in basketball and fencing and staging twenty games of squash each week.

There was one other irritating problem: some members had been taking *men* through the clubhouse. The word went forth that any member or officer seen doing that again would be suspended. "Some members seem to think the Club is Liberty Hall," according to the minutes of one Governors' meeting.

Once the immediate hurdles of opening and staying open had been cleared, the Colony Club began to look to the larger purposes for which it had been founded. Thus began a tradition of public services to society and private attention to the well-being of its own employees, a tradition that continues today.

For instance, in order to help the Club "be the power for good it can be in the community," the Governors announced that on the first Sunday in the month there would be speakers on relevant subjects. In the early years those speakers included:

• The president of the U.S. Mine Workers;
• Woodrow Wilson, then Governor of New Jersey;
• Rabbi Stephen S. Wise;
• Bishop David H. Greer;
• Booker T. Washington;
• Gifford Pinchot, who spoke on conservation of natural resources, which was then not as popular a topic as it is today;

- A panel of twelve experts who discussed "Aims and Problems of Private Schools";
- Lindley M. Garrison, President Wilson's Secretary of War, who told a delighted Colony Club audience in 1912 that he should be known as the "Secretary of Peace," since there had not been a war for so long and would not be one in the foreseeable future;
- General John J. Pershing; and
- Herbert Hoover before he became President.

It is clear from this list that the members of the Colony Club have always been fiercely interested in a wide variety of public issues. Indeed, almost as soon as the Club came into existence it became a force in ways the founders had perhaps not anticipated. A strong stand was taken by many members who believed that it was wrong to own stock in companies that paid dividends at the expense of their employees (low wages, no health insurance, etc.); they gave up such stocks or urged their husbands to dispose of them. Closer to home, a Welfare Committee was formed for the specific purpose of being responsible for the care and needs of the eighty to ninety employees of the Club. When its carpenter contracted TB, for example, he was sent to a sanitarium and his family taken care of until he could return to work.

There was no unemployment insurance, Social Security or welfare in those days. Eventually, a bed was endowed at Presbyterian Hospital for employees of the Club. The Welfare Committee also helped the nine teenagers, fourteen years and older, who were employed as errand boys, to go to night school "so as to be efficient, honest breadwinners," according to Club minutes. One of those so helped eventually became an architect. In addition, the boys were given a two-week vacation in the country "so they would not run wild in the streets of New York."

The Welfare Committee was engaged in other activities as well, such as when it collected $7,000 from members in the early 1900s to give to the Red Cross for earthquake victims in Italy. These victims came from a district that had made a great deal of the lace which was exported to the United States. (In that era lace played an important role in a lady's wardrobe, and among the very first events in the new clubhouse had been a lace exhibit.)

The Governors wished to make the Colony Club "a model and an example of what a club should be from our employees' point of view," according to Club minutes. In 1909, $5,000 was raised to build two sitting rooms on the roof, one for men and one for women, where the employees could rest and read. Maude Adams, the first actress to play the part of Peter Pan and the one who made the play famous, personally donated two armchairs for these rooms. One discriminatory policy remained, however: the men could smoke in their sitting room but the women were not allowed to do so in theirs.

Colonists were also concerned about working conditions in general, especially where women were involved. Mrs. August Belmont, an early Club member and a well-known actress (Eleanor Robson), and many others wanted to hear firsthand about conditions in the factories where "shirtwaist girls," workingwomen, had gone on strike. Against their husbands' advice, the members invited these girls to come to the Colony Club and tell their side of the story. The women spoke of being locked in their workrooms, a situation which had caused many to die in a disastrous fire on the Lower East side.

The members of the Club passed the hat and immediately raised over $5,000 for the striking women. Although the Club remained officially neutral toward the strike, one newspaper called the fundraiser the "first time women of different social ranks had joined forces to benefit womankind."

By 1909 the Colony Club was considered a great success, especially because it had not, as some had predicted, brought about the dissolution of the American family. Miss Marbury, head of the House Committee, believed something great was under way. She predicted that in the not too distant future "women shall be educated to abandon senseless visiting, meaningless gatherings and fictitious and perfunctory pleasure. Our time will be directed to a

Eleanor Robson, an actress, later became Mrs. August Belmont. She has been credited (along with Mrs. John DeWitt Peltz, also a Colony Club member) with saving the Metropolitan Opera during the Depression years.

higher plane of social duty, which duty shall mean our ethical obligations to our neighbor, to our state and to our country."

That the Colony Club provided something that had previously been missing from its members' lives is evident enough from the rapid state of growth in the number of applications over the years from women who wanted to join. In 1910 there were over two hundred women on the waiting list. Sometimes prominence was a key to moving to the head of that list. For instance, Mrs. Grover Cleveland, in spite of her husband's unenlightened views about women's clubs, was moved to the top of the waiting list as soon as she applied.

The activities in which the Colonists engaged in these first decades reflected both the diversity of their own interests and the expanding role of women in all aspects of society. Much was purely recreational. In our earliest days, Club privileges were extended to members of the Ladies' Four-in-Hand Driving Club. These daredevils, dressed (according to the fashion of the times) in large black hats, black veils, long skirts and dusters, drove four- and six-horse teams at breakneck speed up Third Avenue and then raced back down Riverside Drive to the Colony Club.

In 1913 the Club hosted a dog show, but the record does not tell us whether it was open only to very small dogs or whether our eight-pound limit was overlooked just this once.

The members were also involved in world events. When the *Titanic* sank in 1912, the surviving steerage passengers, including many families who had lost their breadwinners, received vital assistance from members of our Club, many of whom had lost personal friends in that tragedy.

As the membership grew, the Colony Club was outgrowing its original quarters. At the same time, the neighborhood around 30th Street and Madison Avenue was changing. Businesses and manufacturing plants were gradually replacing residences. Many of the members who had owned homes in that area, and thus made 120

MRS. WILLIAM H. DEWAR AND THE BARONESS.
Philadelphia Woman Fencing Champion (on the left) and Baroness de
Meyer, Whom She Defeated with Foils in the Colony Club Yesterday.

'ENCING BARONESS LOSES / BOUT TO AMERICAN WOMAN

Defeated in Colony Club and Mrs. Dewar Now Is Champion.

CUP GIVEN BY MRS. WHITNEY

Society Women See First International Match with Foils Ever Staged in America.

Baroness de Meyer was defeated in a fencing bout in the Colony Club by Mrs. William H. Dewar of Philadelphia yesterday. She lost by two touches to one in a contest that was limited to four minutes, but very exciting and fascinating while it lasted. Contrary to expectation, the American style of fencing triumphed over the much heralded European style. Mrs. Dewar was just a bit too agile, too strong of wrist for her titled opponent, and as a result carried off the world's championship and with it a handsome cup given by Mrs. Payne Whitney. The defeat of the Baroness is the first suffered by her since she started on her career

her stand in this country. Baroness de Meyer, whose home is in England, is the European champion, and was considered by foreign experts to be invincible with the foils. Mrs. Dewar is one of the leading woman fencers in this country. She had challenged the Baroness for the world's championship. The gathering was the largest ever brought together in any local club to watch a fencing bout.

Before coming to this country the Baroness was the amateur championship of England, France, Germany and Italy, the best fellowswomen of those countries having fallen prey to her expert blade.

Although Mrs. Dewar is not recognized as the American champion there being no American title holder, she is regarded as the peer of any fencewoman in this country with the exception of Silvi Marston of Leland Stanford University of California, considered by American experts the equal of the Philadelphian. Miss Marston was one of the challengers of the Baroness, but the Colony Club refused to sanction the bout, the club officials deciding Miss Marston a professional.

The defeat at the hands of Mrs. Dewar almost caused Baroness de Meyer to go into hysterics. So sure was she of winning that she lost control of her steel after Mrs. Dewar gained the first touch. She couldn't understand how an American woman who has never before engaged in a bout of any importance could get past her guard. It became apparent to the spectators that Mrs. Dewar would meet the laurels after the first touch was scored, the Baroness being unnerved at the calmness of her less experienced opponent. Although Mrs. Dewar continued to hold the foil with marked steadiness, after the first touch the Baroness guided her blade with trembling hands.

One and a half minutes after the bout was started, the Baroness clashed her

Mrs. William H. Dewar, who defeated European Champion Baroness de Meyer with foils, in the Colony Club Match in 1912, became the new champion.

Mrs. Arthur Iselin driving, accompanied by Mrs. Theodore Roosevelt, Miss Ruth Twombly, Mrs. Goadby Loew, Miss Angelica Gerry, Miss Harriet Alexander (who became Mrs. Winthrop Aldrich) and Mrs. Belmont Tiffany. They are fighting a stiff breeze off Riverside Drive (their hats securely fastened with dark veils) as they return to their starting point—the Colony Club.

Madison Avenue a sensible location for them to meet, were selling their brownstone houses and moving uptown. New, tall buildings were casting their shadows across the clubhouse, and at one meeting it was sorrowfully noted that a bus stop had been installed outside the front door.

By January 1914, when the Governors decided to increase the membership from 750 to 1,200, it was clear that it was time to move to bigger and more appropriately situated quarters. The big question, of course, was: Where? A number of sites, such as 66th Street between Lexington and Third, 65th and Madison and 54th and Park, were considered. For a while a spot at 42nd and Park Avenue, the ''Chapin plot,'' was tentatively chosen, and in fact, architects and decorators were hired with that location in mind, but the Governors eventually voted against it. By a margin of one vote, the Governors selected Park Avenue and 62nd Street as the second home of the Colony Club.

Our first clubhouse is still standing and has been declared a landmark building by the City of New York. It is now the home of The American Academy of Dramatic Arts, which for many years used our old swimming pool as a storage area for its costumes.

Two

THE SECOND CLUBHOUSE

BY THE FALL of 1914 the hardships of the war in Europe were making themselves felt in America, and the Governors voted to give members a little longer to pay their dues, particularly those members who had volunteered their services in Europe. Plans for the new clubhouse, however, continued. The Georgian Room on exhibition at Schmids was purchased, and noted designer Robert W. Chanler was commissioned to paint murals in the loggia.

The Governors were surprised when, after the plans designed by Delano and Aldrich for the new clubhouse were made public, only twelve women appeared at the meeting that was scheduled for discussion of the project (and none of the twelve this time noticed in the blueprints the too-small food elevator from the kitchen to the ballroom!). A few years earlier, Club officials had been complaining that nobody was putting anything in the Complaint Box. Annoyed by the paltry turnout at the meeting, the secretary remarked pointedly, ''A thousand other members are now honor bound to refrain from later criticism.''

This poor turnout must have reflected general satisfaction with the plans of the architects and the Governors rather than apathy on the part of the membership, because the following year the Governors reported that they were grateful for the smooth, efficient way the move from the old clubhouse to the new had been ac-

The present clubhouse at 62nd Street and Park Avenue was opened to the members in 1915.

complished. Everyone liked the work done by Mesdames Nicholas and Hughes. The legions of armchair skeptics, primarily male, had insisted that women could not work together in large numbers without friction. How wrong they were!

While the broad strokes of Colony Club affairs, such as moving from one home to another, deserve a good deal of attention, we should not neglect the many other, smaller elements that, taken together, made the Colony Club what it is today.

The Loggia, with the famous ceiling murals by Robert W. Chanler, as it looked circa 1915. He was not satisfied with his first murals and redid them. It is now the members' dining room.

The front hall. The doormen are in their summer uniforms circa 1920.

THE NEW CLUBHOUSE LOUNGE DECORATED IN CHINTZ

At the Executive Committee meeting in March, 1919, a special group was appointed to purchase "new chintz" for the lounge. Despite early interest in decoration of the Club, starting with Elsie DeWolfe, it was not until 1960 that a Decorating Committee was established. Mrs. John B. Trevor, its first chairman, and Mrs. Reginald P. Rose were responsible for the style of the lounge as we know it today. Subsequent Committees—one of the Club's most active groups—continue to maintain the beauty and comfort in the clubhouse.

For instance, the Club boasted some fine squash players, such as founding treasurer Miss Anne Morgan (daughter of financier J.P. Morgan, who was on our first men's advisory board) and Bostonian Miss Eleanor Sears. The Club awarded $500 in prizes to the top players each year. We shone in fencing, too; in 1912 our team beat a top European squad. One pivotal match pitted Mrs. William Dewar against an opponent named Baroness de Meer. When Mrs. Dewar won, the Colonists of the New World scored a minor triumph over the nobility of the Old.

The first-floor main entrance to the ballroom as it looked on our Seventy-Fifth Diamond Jubilee, November 30, 1978.

Those who had artistic tendencies took over the clubhouse one night in the spring of 1916, banishing all male employees for the evening and staging a "theatrical evening." The New York *Evening Post* carried an item about the performances, which must have been fairly exotic if the casting of Emma B. Auchincloss as a Spanish bandit and Margaret M. Petersen as an Algerian prince is any indication.

In 1917 roller-skating, golf and reducing lessons were added to the activities (and in the 1920s mah-jong became popular)—but you couldn't start a card game in the clubhouse after 11:45 p.m.— nor was doubling at bridge allowed to continue past 100 points a trick.

The members of the Colony Club continued to be deeply interested and involved in the affairs of the world at large. Most members, led by Mrs. Clarence MacKay, Mrs. O.H.P. Belmont (the former Mrs. William K. Vanderbilt) and Mrs. Robert Marsh were active suffragettes, working to gain women the right to vote. Detachments would leave the clubhouse in an open touring car to canvass passers-by for donations to the movement, and sometimes men would shout at them, "Go home to your children!" The Colonists would answer back, "You don't say that to women working in the factories or to actresses in the theater!"

When the United States entered World War I in 1917, the Colony Club became fully mobilized. The Club's gymnasium was turned into a workroom, and both Colonists and their chauffeurs set to work knitting for the Red Cross, using wool that had been donated by members. Members wore velvet dresses to save woolen cloth for the soldiers and sailors. Operating costs were cut by more than a third, and some of the savings were used to buy an ambulance and send it to Europe. Anne Morgan sent a second ambulance on her own and then went to France herself to see what she could do on the scene. Later she was joined by other Colonists,

Mabel P. Smithers and Ada Gibb Hester as Disraeli and Queen Victoria, circa 1916.

Emma B. Auchincloss as a "Spanish Bandit."

Rachel Crothers, famous author, as a ballet dancer with a member dressed as a nun.

including our first president, Mrs. J. Borden Harriman and Miss Sarah Larkin, who later became Mrs. Albert Loening.

These efforts did not end with the war as far as the Colonists were concerned. The president reported, "The Club is now a quiet refuge, where members, exhausted from war work and their efforts for the poor of Europe, can come." The Club offered a "slim menu" in the dining room at lunchtime: the portions were smaller but the prices were the same as usual (75¢ to $1.50), with the difference going to help feed Europe's hungry children.

By instituting a temporary membership category for foreigners, the Colony Club did what it could to combat the xenophobia that a painful foreign war had created in many Americans. The following passage is from the minutes of the meeting at which the vote on the new category was taken:

> It seems likely now that many foreigners will come to us (up to now we have gone to Paris, London or Rome) and that we, in welcoming our foreign guests, represent that old Colonial spirit which we choose to identify ourselves with when we call ourselves the "Colony Club."

This warm policy to foreigners has continued to the present in the form of our Honorary Visitors Committee.

During these years the Colony Club held a conference on socialism, and among the many interesting lectures was one called "Buddhism to Modern Thought." Many members signed up for a course on American Government. A series of lectures entitled "Problems of the Day" was particularly popular. There was even an occasional ideological clash. Some members protested vehemently when Max Eastman, editor of the Communist newspaper *The Masses*, was invited to lecture, but the Governors stood firm: Mr. Eastman could speak, they ruled, as long as someone with opposing views was also engaged.

In 1919 modern art still shocked even the most sophisticated New Yorkers, but the Colony Club was again ahead of its time when Gertrude Vanderbilt Whitney and other members put together a showing of new artwork in the clubhouse, which included their own artistic endeavors.

Those early Colonists were tolerant: non-members were first known as "strangers" but were soon reclassified as "guests." The early members were thrifty: the extra grease produced in the clubhouse kitchen was sold, adding seven or eight dollars each month to the coffers.

And sometimes they were even daring. In April 1920 the Governors voted to allow members to use the swimming pool without wearing bathing suits—if, as mentioned in the minutes, "it wasn't overdone!" This was quite a step for a club that had been conceived in 1900 in Newport by women enshrouded in modest bathing suits and long black stockings.

A minor controversy in the 1920s threatened to become a major one when someone said there should be a radio in the clubhouse so members could listen to Charlie McCarthy, W.C. Fields and Will Rogers. The proposal was voted down in favor of the Club's home-grown entertainment. This was often as imaginative as any radio program. One example was a series of evening functions with titles such as "Colonial Evening," "Chinese Evening," "Soiree de Type Imagine," and "Eighteenth Century Italian Evening," each presumably complete with corresponding costumes, cuisine and entertainment.

The Colony Club was so successful, and its management so skilled and efficient, that at the Club's Twentieth Annual Meeting in April 1924, the president, Miss Ruth Morgan addressed the question "Can women really run a club?" by paying this tribute to the Governors:

> Twenty-one representatives of the Club, a constantly changing group, have answered this question, developing not only all the activities represented in a men's club, but many more of which men had never thought. This has caused many thousands of men within the past two years to ask, "How is it done?"

The president, noting that in 1903 the Colony Club had had a men's advisory committee, said that now, in 1924, perhaps there ought to be a *women's* advisory committee to guide the *men's* clubs!

By 1925 the waiting list had grown to over 1,000. Mrs. Rodman Montgomery, aged nineteen when she applied, was told that she would have to wait for forty-three years in spite of the fact that her grandmother was a founding member. To prevent a competing club from being formed, the Governors announced that eventually 240 from that group of prospective members would be invited to join. It was a shrewd strategy: since each of these applicants had an equal chance of soon becoming a Colonist, few of them were inclined to remove their names from consideration and join some other club.

Colonists also excelled in forensics. In 1926 the Junior League challenged us to a debate on the question "Does genius have a moral obligation?" When we won for the third straight time, the Club president, Mrs. Seymour Cromwell, grandly reported:

> The wit and intelligence of the Junior League is no match for the mental adroitness and resourcefulness of our Colony Club teams. And no one can doubt that as a group we are the most financially astute, the most intelligent and intellectual, the most beautiful, and the most elegant.

In 1927 our annual report included this hopeful passage: "The period of intolerance in this country is passing. Perhaps in some small way we of the Colony Club have helped to restore the generous attitude of mind which must remain the American ideal and the basis of American institutions."

The Colony Club along with the rest of America had a prosperous, carefree time during the Roaring Twenties. In 1921 the president, Miss Ruth Morgan, happily reported, "The whole financial situation of the Colony Club is so much better than any of the *men's* clubs that [it] has been repeatedly consulted as to what *we* would advise them to do, a proud reversal from our former humble position of seeking advice from them."

Many were concerned that Americans during the 1920s were recoiling from the crisis of the last decade by becoming indolent and overly extravagant. In an annual report, the Governors noted with dismay: "Now the average American woman between thirty and forty refuses to allow the mantle of the pioneer feminist to fall on her lazy shoulders; or to respond to the battle cries that got women into causes."

However, the Governors did not believe this statement applied to Colony Club women. In fact, it was noted at the time of the Silver

Frances Perkins was Secretary of Labor under President Franklin D. Roosevelt. She was the first woman to serve in the United States Cabinet.

Lucrezia Bori, a leading singer of the Metropolitan Opera in the 1930s, sang her favorite song "Marie Antoinette" at the Club's Fiftieth Anniversary Celebration.

Helen Wills Moody was the outstanding women's tennis player during the 1930s. She was known on the courts as "Little Miss Poker Face" and famous for the words "I have brawn not brains."

Ethel Barrymore, actress and sister of John and Lionel Barrymore, was known at the Colony Club for giving fascinating dinners for eight women (never six or ten, nor did she ever include any men).

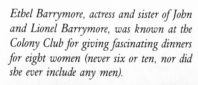

Jubilee in 1928 that "the younger women [in the Club] seemed to understand and appreciate what the older members had done."

The youngest set had apparently been forgiven for their high jinks in the gym a quarter-century before, by the way, because small children of members were cordially invited to the Twenty-Fifth Anniversary celebration, the Silver Jubilee. (The invitation to the Twenty-Fifth Silver Anniversary celebration was found in the archives of the Museum of the City of New York in 1978, and the enchanting picture from the invitation was used again on the Seventy-Fifth Anniversary program of our Fashion Revue.)

After this decade of plenty came the Depression, a time of scarcity and sacrifice, and the Colony Club also shared in these along with the rest of the country. Our mortgage was paid off by the spring of 1931, three years ahead of time, and not a moment too soon—the Depression meant a loss to the Club of $65,000 a year in entertainment income alone. Since athletics were considered a luxury, the gym was empty. Nonetheless, we managed to tighten our belt, stay in the black and still keep a full membership, though some who could no longer afford their dues resigned and wrote, "When times get better we hope to be reinstated."

With the start of World War II in 1939 in Poland, our gym was again transformed into a workroom, this time under the supervision of Mrs. William Jay Schieffelin. Over $80,000 was raised to pay for supplies and other costs. Roller-skating lessons were replaced by sewing lessons, and during the war we shipped 121,000 garments overseas, produced at a cost of fifty cents each. We made over a half-million surgical dressings. Classes were held by the Red Cross and the American Women Volunteer Service. Colonists and staff members enlisted in both the military and voluntary services. The Colonists' shifting priorities during the war were evident in their decisions about how best to use clubhouse space. We lost our two squash courts; they became part of the accounting office. Part of the gymnasium became bedrooms and the rest was used for storage. Fortunately, a section of the gymnasium was rediscovered during our Seventy-Fifth Anniversary and then turned into our much-needed exercise room by our vice-president, Mrs. Cochran B. Supplee, and the Bath and Athletic Committee.

In 1953 we celebrated our Club's Golden Jubilee. The history of the Club was told decade by decade, illustrated by different tableaux

WORLD WAR II

The gymnasium was turned into a workroom for the war effort under Mrs. William Jay Schieffelin, who chaired a large committee of Colony Club members. Please note the exercise pulleys on our gym wall.

FIFTIETH ANNIVERSARY 1953

Chorus of pioneers who opened the show by singing "Merry Oldsmobile, My Automobile."

Mrs. Richard Aldrich	Mrs. Harry T. Peters
Mrs. Francis C. Bishop	Mrs. J. H. Philbin
Mrs. F. Higginson Cabot	Mrs. Alan T. Schumacher
Mrs. Edward Delafield	Mrs. Robert D. Sterling .
Mrs. Lloyd Griscom	Mrs. John B. Trevor, Jr.
Miss Dorothy H. McGee	Miss Agnes Graham Troup
Mrs. Clarence Mitchell	Mrs. Allen Tucker

on a makeshift stage. Mrs. John Marsh, vice-president, was chairman of the event with Mrs. Reginald Rose, our president, ex-officio.

During the fifties, there was an uproar in the Club such as had never been seen or heard before. What caused it was the suggestion to the Board by a group of prominent members that *men* be allowed to stay overnight at the Club—with their wives, of course! Mrs.

FIFTIETH ANNIVERSARY 1953

Former presidents at supper: (LEFT TO RIGHT) Mrs. Langbourne M. Williams, Jr., Mrs. Henry James, Mrs. J. Borden Harriman, and the then-current president, Mrs. Reginald P. Rose, with member Mrs. Richard Tobin at the extreme right.

They are waiting for former-presidents Mrs. Seymour Cromwell and Mrs. Montgomery Hare.

A scene from World War I workroom as shown in the anniversary pageant. Mrs. Green is holding the umbrella which she is about to carry in the suffrage parade. Workers are Mrs. Duncan Harris, Mrs. J. Horton Ijams, Mrs. Barents Lefferts and Mrs. William J. Schieffelin.

JUNIOR MEMBERS

Miss Julia Beals, Mrs. Joseph Devine, Miss Elisabeth Nelidow, Miss Patricia Ripley and Mrs. Harold H. Healy, Jr. are discussing why they joined the Colony Club with Mrs. August Belmont.

Rose, fortunately a calm and fair president, was beseiged by both sides. Finally the proposal was passed as a six-month experiment, but it was evident that the vast majority of the members approved and the experiment became a permanent policy.

Although we had junior members eighteen years of age and older, for some years there was no formal committee for them. In researching our history I found that one member, Mrs. Harold H. Healy, had started two of our ''new'' committees—the Younger Members Committee and the Lending Library Committee. Therefore, I have asked her to tell about the beginning of these two committees in her own words:

In early 1963 the Board of Governors of the Colony Club decided that, as there was a growing number of younger members in the Club, more activities of special interest should be provided for this group.

The Younger Members Committee was composed of members under forty years of age. During the first year we had four major events.

To start us off in the fall, we had a luncheon-lecture in the Ballroom with Harold Prince, the young director/producer of *West Side Story*, *Pajama Game* and *Damn Yankees* fame.

In December we had Christmas carols in the lounge for members, their children and grandchildren. It was very festive, with the children sitting on the floor in front of the Christmas tree. The singing was led by a member of the committee with a beautiful soprano voice accompanied by another committee member playing her golden harp. Other committee members took turns reading from the Christmas story and it was charming to hear the children reciting the passages with them.

The next event was the Butterfly Ball in the spring. It was a dinner dance held in the Ballroom, which was delightfully decorated with butter-flies by a member of the committee.

The final planned activity for the year was a complete tour of the club-house from the wine cellars to the roof, a tour which was very enlight-ening to us all.

Our first newsletter was printed on pink paper to attract attention. It was sent to all members under forty years of age to stimulate their interest in coming to the Club more often and in using its facilities, which in-cluded the inexpensive sandwich menu in the Members' Dining Room started by the committee.

This was the beginning of the Younger Members Committee. It has been brilliantly carried forward to become an integral part of the Club, as well as a great asset.

Ten years later, in 1974, the Governors asked me, as chairman of the Library Committee, to form a lending library for the members of the Club. The committee proceeded slowly during the first year in estab-lishing rules and regulations, and in explaining these procedures to the members.

From this beginning developing a Circulating Library run on the honor system. Members of the Club who wished to borrow books paid a small fee to become members of the library. This money enabled the committee to buy newly published and current books each month for the Circulating Library. As a bonus, two free lectures were given each year for library members only. It was easy to find speakers among our noted author-members and other distinguished members of the Club. These talks are held in the Library itself and are most interesting and stimulating.

The committee, as volunteers, ran the library. Once a year a book sale for the whole Club was held. The out-of-date and older books were sold in order to make room for the newer books in our limited space of four bookstands. These sales proved to be very popular with the members.

The Library Room is restricted to Club members, who can take advantage of the many interesting magazines, periodicals and table books displayed for their enjoyment as well as the quiet seclusion in which they can write or study.

The Library is a delightful place to spend an extra half-hour or so, happily presided over by our mascots, the two famous cherub figures on the mantel shelf, named "Reading" and "Writing."

These two new committees added greatly to the enjoyment of life members of the Club during the otherwise difficult, tragic Vietnam years. In the 1960s the Club continued to provide a great many diverse programs. Senator Barry Goldwater addressed the membership in 1962, two years before he became a candidate for the presidency. In 1971, Colonel Frank Borman described his Apollo moon flight to the largest crowd ever assembled at the Colony Club.

It is true that in the sixties several young members tried to arrive dressed in blue jeans, but this minor Colony Club revolution was nipped in the bud. It was not until our president, Mrs. Hermann Place, arrived in a beautiful tailored pants suit and jacket that elegant pants suits were allowed and appreciated.

The seventies brought many new ventures, which have continued to be successful in the eighties.

In 1975, Mrs. Hugh Bullock founded the Honorary Visitors Committee. This committee was formed to be helpful to wives of diplomats to the United States and to the United Nations, who are acquainted with members of the Club. They are elected to a temporary honorary membership by the Board of Governors. Recently this group has included several women who are diplomats in their own right. Their presence in the Club has added greatly to the membership.

The Decorating Committee renovated and redecorated our beautiful ballroom, which became the scene for the new and popular Candlelight Dinners. As service at home grows more difficult these gala occasions enable our members to entertain easily and frequently in the gracious atmosphere of our Club.

During the seventies the Card Committee expanded its program to include lessons for every level of bridge player. The interest in card playing has greatly increased and duplicate bridge has recently been added.

The Gift Boutique within the Hairdressing Department was expanded with many new and attractive gifts, proving a source of pleasure and convenience for our members.

Responding to requests for more exercise, classes began in our new gymnasium, including body education and dance exercise. This trend toward more exercise continued, with ballet and yoga classes being added. In 1984 a complete renovation of our Bath Department was done to include a sauna and more fitness equipment. How pleased our first president, Mrs. Harriman, would be to see our renewed interest in athletics.

Three

1978
THE SEVENTY-FIFTH ANNIVERSARY
AND PRESENT TIMES

AND SUDDENLY it was 1978, and we were seventy-five years old (or young).

We agreed we had a reputation, but at seventy-five years of age, did we still have the same energy and imagination, the talent and concern for others that was displayed by our founders?

Our Diamond Jubilee answered that question. A committee of nineteen (which grew to several hundred) decided that there should be an open house on November 30th, followed by a fashion revue on December 7th.

Mrs. Edward Chase and Mrs. Philip Wiedel were the overall chairmen with Mrs. Charles I. Pierce, president, serving ex officio. Mrs. Mary Hope Lewis and Mrs. John Hardy were in charge of the open house, while Mrs. Howard Cox, with the assistance of Mrs. Reginald Rose, planned the Fashion Revue, which would also illustrate our history.

The Revue was brilliantly staged by Mrs. Cope Walbridge, vice-chairman of the Fashion Revue. A movie of this event was produced by Miss Charlotte McKim, vice-chairman of the Younger Members Committee.

For the open house evening reception on November 30th, 1978, an Edwardian Ballroom was created by Mrs. Leicester van Leer and her Flower Committee with enormous palms and plants on loan from the Botanical Garden. The clubhouse was filled with extraordinary and beautiful Christmas decorations made and hung by Mrs. Frederick Houston much earlier than usual. An elaborate and continuous Edwardian buffet was planned by Mrs. John Tilney and her Food Committee for a record number of members and guests. There were 759 attendees who danced to two orchestras playing waltzes and other "turn of the century" music, and were entertained by a puppet show and a prestidigitator. Our beautiful pool was open and looked enchanting with its floating candles. The entire clubhouse was aglow and the beauty and spirit of this memorable evening would have delighted our founding members.

We had to start the Fashion Revue somewhere, so a postcard was sent out to all members asking for clothes, corsets, nightcaps, purses, and any articles of clothing or accessories dating from 1900 to the present. Boxes poured in. We were overwhelmed. Realizing the value of these items, we asked the curator from the Costume Institute at the Metropolitan Museum, Stella Blum, and its top costume restorer, Elizabeth Lawrence, to come and examine the clothes.

They arrived one hot and humid August day and were shown to the old squash court, which had no ventilation but was the only place we had at that time to store the various articles. They were ecstatic when they saw the garments and asked if the Metropolitan could have many of them for its famous collection after our show.

Mrs. J. Warner Butterworth, an author and member of the Younger Members Committee, wrote the following account of the Seventy-Fifth Anniversary and describes what the Colony Club has meant to her.

Fearless, loyal, gracious and very feminine—words from the obituary of the Colony Club member Alice Damrosch Kiaer. Fearless and loyal are words seldom used for women, even those who, like Mrs. Kiaer, scale mountains and win races. They are qualities long thought to be the prerogatives of men. We tend to forget that they apply as well to women

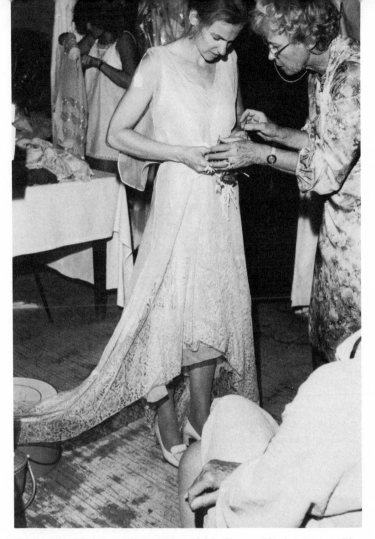

The "start" of the planned Fashion Revue for the Seventy-fifth Anniversary. Mrs. Harald S. de Ropp is trying on a dress to get the size (in early days dresses were made to order without clear sizes) with the assistance of Mrs. Howard E. Cox.

Mrs. J. Warner Butterworth is in the background deciding which is "back or front." At extreme lower right, partially hidden, sits the chief restorer from the Costume Institute of the Metropolitan Museum telling us which clothes she would like for the permanent collection of the museum. The scene is June 1978 in the unventilated squash court.

like Mrs. Kiaer and countless other athletes, journalists, scientists, poets, settlement house workers and suffragettes who were and are members of our Club.

Separated from fearless and loyal, gracious and feminine are easily trivialized into an ineffectual froth of ruffles and careful smiles. United, these words tell as much about what it means to be a woman in 1983 as they did in 1903.

For those of us who grew up in the fifties and sixties, it seemed natural to turn to men for our role models. They were the lawyers, scientists, poets, bankers and politicians we wanted to be. Theirs were the faces we saw in our magazines and newspapers and on our television sets.

There were not many models of mature women for us to follow on television then or now. It was the men's voices we heard from the podiums of our graduations, their exploits we read about in our history books. For those of us who went to coed colleges, there was little chance to know women of different generations. Afterwards, as we pursued our careers, men were our employers and role models.

In March of 1978, I was asked to join the Seventy-Fifth Anniversary Fashion and Historical Revue Committee. It was the first time I had served on a committee made up exclusively of women—women ranging in age from their twenties to their eighties. It was for me a unique and memorable experience. During the next sixteen months I came to know and admire this remarkable group.

Our task was to plan an appropriate celebration for this important anniversary. Under the leadership of Mrs. Howard E. Cox, the history of the Colony Club was researched. As we looked through old minutes, books and newspaper clippings, names like Elsie de Wolfe, Katherine Cornell, Cornelia Otis Skinner, Mrs. J. Borden Harriman, Mrs. Dwight Morrow (acting president of Smith), Congressman Ruth Pratt, Eleanor Roosevelt, Mrs. Ogden Reid, Mrs. Sherman P. Haight, Kitty Carlisle Hart slowly took on life.

We got to know the women who marched with the suffragettes, as well as the women who did the Charleston; the women who ran for Congress; the women who sent errand boys to night school and on vacations in the country; the women who landscaped gardens; and the women who flew to South America with Lindbergh and collected fossils in the Pearl Islands; the operatic sopranos and the journalists; the first women amateur fencing champion and even the woman who rode the elevator every day to the top floor and then walked down the stairs backwards for exercise!

Mrs. Reginald P. Rose (CENTER) and Mrs. Howard E. Cox (LEFT), commentators at the dress rehearsal of the Fashion Revue, with Mrs. Philip D. Wiedel (RIGHT).

We determined to tell the stories we had learned in the form of a pageant. It would be made up of scenes from the history of our Club. Members would model clothes owned by their predecessors, and these clothes, beginning with the bustles and hobble skirts of the early 1900s, would help tell of the changes that had occurred in the ensuing decades. As we collected clothes and accessories, each detail was checked for historical accuracy by representatives from the Costume Institute of the Metropolitan Museum.

The pageant began with a regal entrance by Mrs. Harold Healy playing the part of our first president, Mrs. J. Borden Harriman. She was dressed in a magnificent black velvet gown by Worth, similar to the one worn by Mrs. Harriman in her portrait. There were early Club meetings, a 1905 wedding—complete with flower girls and grandmère-athletes in bloomers and linen croquet skirts, women depicting suffragettes, and others in World War I uniforms.

Next came the Poirets and "the dancing daughters," sequined flappers

Mrs. Harold H. Healy, Jr. standing in front of Mrs. J. Borden Harriman's portrait. Mrs. Healy opened the Fashion Revue portraying Mrs. Harriman, our first president.

Waiting in the hallway to go on the runway in the Ballroom. Mrs. John Cutrer Smith is in the black lace dress her grandfather, Mr. George Allen, brought back from Paris for her grandmother about eighty years ago.

"Charlestoning" down the runway. The gardenias and Vionnets of the thirties and the glamorous nights of Charles James and Schaparelli gave way to Rosie the Riveter and our Marine Colonel Ruth Streeter (Mrs. Thomas W.), and also war correspondent Candace Van Alen (Mrs. James) and WAVE Lt. Jane Darlington Irwin (Mrs. Charles) of World War II.

After the war came the Balenciagas, Diors and Mainbochers, and the fairytale romance of the deb dresses of leading black designer Anne Lowe. They in turn gave way to the minis and the jeans and the pants suits of the sixties and the seventies. Through each decade marched the indomnitable Mrs. Colony Club, enacted by Mrs. Peter Nicholas, changing her hat and hemline to match the time, but not her basic dark suit, white gloves, nor her striking presence or dignified determination!

As the concept of the pageant slowly evolved through long hot summer days and cold winter days, from the selecting and cataloguing of clothes in the cramped quarters of the old squash court to the late rehearsals in the ballroom and its final fruition on the runway on December 7, 1978, so did my concept of the Colony Club and its members.

Not only did I learn about the Worths, Vionnets, Diors and Balenciagas, but I came to know the hopes and aspirations of the women who wore them and their amazing diversity of interest and achievement. For the first time I began to think that perhaps we are lawyers, scientists, bankers and politicians today not only because of the male role models we sought to emulate, but also because of these strong, determined and innovative women who were our forebears.

Women's clubhouses tend to be dingy holes-in-the-wall compared to their male counterparts, but the Colony Club, its building and location, its pure solid architectural beauty, is not only a tribute to the taste and intelligence of our predecessors, but, more than that, it is a strong statement on the importance of women.

The fencers, gymnasts, swimmers and horsewomen of the past taught us to care for our bodies and provided us with the pool and gymnasium we use today. The archaeologists, astronomers and scholars taught us to keep our minds equally well tuned.

And, as I walk through the gallery of distinguished members with my mother and daughter, or browse through the shelves of books written by members in the library, I realize that unlike the male faces I see at my university club, these faces are all female. These are the faces I want my daughter to see and know so that when she grows up she will know women to be "fearless and loyal" as well as "gracious and feminine."

WORLD WAR II

Mrs. John W. Mackay is in an A.W.V.S. uniform representing the hundreds of Colony Club members who volunteered for the A.W.V.S., the Red Cross and other organizations that helped the war effort.

Lt. Jane Darlington Irwin is representing the Colony Club members who served in the armed forces. Jane Darlington enlisted when the Waves had not yet gotten their name.

Col. Ruth Cheney Streeter is in her World War II Marine uniform. She became the top ranking woman officer of the U.S.M.C.W.R.

Candace Alig Van Alen served overseas in World War II as a war correspondent for International News Service. Her headquarters were in Paris through 1946. In 1947 she became an editorial writer for the New York Herald Tribune.

Mrs. "Colony Club" (Mrs. Peter Nicholas) who never forsook her dark blue suit, hat, and white gloves all through the seventy-five years of the Fashion Revue. She is chastising and chasing Mrs. Cochran B. Supplee off the 1950 runway, telling her not to come back in a pant suit until the 1960s!

FLAPPERS FROM THE "ROARING TWENTIES"

(LEFT TO RIGHT)
Mrs. Ann Stanton Maulsby, Secretary of the Club
Mrs. Mary Hope Lewis Ford, Assistant Treasurer of the Club
Mrs. Charles F. Morgan, Treasurer of the Club

Our Seventy-Fifth Anniversary did many things for our Club. Besides making us proud of our early founders, the Seventy-Fifth led to many friendships between the older and the younger members. Many younger members told me that before the anniversary they would often tiptoe into the Club holding their breath, afraid of annoying one of the elders. But with such a large number of older and younger members working together in close, hectic quarters toward a common goal, the formal barriers of the three-generation gap broke down. In their place were new friendships and a mutual appreciation of each generation's many talents.

To sum up over eighty years of history of a group of women as dynamic and as multifaceted as the members of the Colony Club is an almost impossible task. I could, of course, end with what the Club itself has meant to me personally, but I suspect that this would not tell enough of the story. Instead, I have asked some of my fellow members to let me have some of their thoughts about the Colony Club.

• • •

This is what Mrs. Edward T. Chase, a member of the Literature and Art Committee (responsible for the selection of speakers) for the last sixteen years, eight of them as chairman, wrote for our history:

The Colony Club, with its incomparable staff, superb cuisine and graceful, classical spaces is a kind of miraculous distillation of a great country house which we all experience gratefully and joyfully share with our family and friends.

The perfect Delano Ballroom evokes happy memories of decades of great occasions in our lives—wedding receptions, our daughters' debut dances, childrens' dancing classes and anniversary celebrations.

And within these hospitable walls we gather for lectures, on *and* off the record, by distinguished members and by an array of national and international personages such as ambassadors, diplomats, publishers, bankers, journalists, economics, directors of the major American museums and other cultural institutions—all speakers who reflect the tremendous range of members' interests and activities.

The platform of the Colony Club has been sought because of the high regard in which its discerning audience is held. In recent years we have been instructed, enlightened and amused by many memorable speakers, among them the following:

• Osborn Elliott, former editor of *Newsweek*, who spoke on "New York City's Unemployment Problems";

• Mrs. Vincent Astor spoke on "Developing a Foundation Policy";

• Mr. Thomas Hoving, former director of the Metropolitan Museum, spoke on "The Tomb of Tutankhamen";

• Mr. Louis Auchincloss, lawyer, author and past president of the Museum of the City of New York, spoke on "Manhattan—1903";

• Mr. Jay Iselin, president of Channel 13, spoke on "Public Broadcasting Today and Tomorrow";

• Mr. Daniel P. Davison, president of U.S. Trust Co., spoke on "The Enemy of the Rich";

• Dr. S. Dillon Ripley of the Smithsonian Institution spoke on "Our Government and Our Culture: A Dilemma";

• Dr. George Gallup, chairman of the Gallup Poll, spoke on "New Factors in the Coming Election";

• Betty Sherrill of McMillen, Inc., spoke on "What's Going On in Decorating";

• Mr. William C. Colby, former director of the U.S. Central Intelligence Agency, spoke on "Intelligence for the 1980s";

• Jill Ker Conway, president of Smith College, spoke on "Mothers, Daughters and Superwoman";

• Mr. Thomas J. Watson, Jr., former U.S. Ambassador to Russia and past president of International Business Machines, spoke on "Nuclear Arms and the Soviet Union";

• Jane Brody, health editor of *The New York Times*, spoke on "How to Stop Dieting *and Lose* Weight; and

• Francis Thorne (composer and pianist) playing Irving Berlin.

• • •

And here are the thoughts of Mrs. Peter H. Nicholas, who so mischievously and handsomely portrayed Mrs. Colony Club through all the decades at our Seventy-Fifth Anniversary celebration:

V.I.P.s AT THE SEVENTY-FIFTH ANNIVERSARY LUNCHEON
DECEMBER 7, 1978

(ABOVE, LEFT TO RIGHT)

Mrs. Peter Van Ness Philip, *Vice Chairman of the House Committee (now, 1984, Secretary of the Club)*

Mrs. William Ward Foshay, *former First Vice President*

Mrs. John B. Marsh, *Archivist and a former First Vice President for 18 years (1952–1970)*

Mrs. Gordon Rentschler, *former President*

Mrs. Charles I. Pierce, *President*

Mrs. Reginald P. Rose, *former President*

Mrs. Louis Reynal, *former House Committee Chairman*

(OPPOSITE, LEFT TO RIGHT)

Mrs. John S. Tilney, *Chairman of the Food Committee*

Mrs. Walter S. Gifford, *former President*

Mrs. Edward T. Chase, *Chairman of the Committee on Literature and Art*

Mrs. Robert DeVecchi, *former Chairman of the Committee on Literature and Art*

Mrs. L. Robertson Hatch, *former Chairman of the Baths and Athletics Committee*

Mrs. Hugh Bullock, *Chairman of the Honorary Visitors Committee*

(CLOCKWISE FROM BOTTOM LEFT)

Mrs. William Everdell III, Governor

Mrs. William B. Given, Jr., former First and Second Vice President, and
  former Treasurer of the Club for 13 years (1956–1967)

Mrs. Philip Wiedel, Governor, Co-Chairman of the Seventy-fifth Anniversary
  Committee

Mrs. Robert J. Lewis, former President

Mrs. Hugh E. Paine, former Second Vice President

(OPPOSITE)

This photograph was taken at our Seventy-fifth Anniversary Fashion Revue. Mrs. Walter A. Kernan, who has served as First and Second Vice President and Treasurer, and Mrs. Winthrop Rutherfurd are accompanied by their daughter (and daughter-in-law), Mrs. Winthrop Rutherfurd, Jr. and her three daughters, Elizabeth Polk Rutherfurd, Leslie Hadden Rutherfurd and Emily Kernan Rutherfurd.

The children's great-grandmothers, Mrs. Hamilton Hadden and Mrs. Frank Lyon Polk, were both Governors of the Colony Club. Mr. Frank Lyon Polk was the Club's first lawyer and responsible for its incorporation.

The Colony Club has been seen by many outsiders from only one perspective: that of a club exclusively for women from the older, more affluent families of New York City and their children. In the Club, members were perceived as gathering for social events or resting from volunteer activities confined mostly to the "do-good" areas.

We cannot worry about yesterday, nor about tomorrow's inadequate view of our "home away from home," but it is incumbent upon the present members to articulate for others the qualities that make membership in the Colony Club a quietly prized possession.

This Club imposes nothing, provides all for our comfort and in its quiet interior allows for the easy flow of stellar events, social and artistic and intellectual. All the activities are abetted by a staff, which does its job as if it were its own pleasure it was serving: always courteous, cheerful, caring and attentive—and in this day and age, a wonder of efficiency, precision and command.

The atmosphere of the Club is quiet and hushed between events, which is comforting to nerves shattered by the incessant, intrusive cacophony of our rude city. Its atmosphere is serene, graceful and, above all, tasteful and elegant in its appointments and services. This is due to a marked degree to a Board of Governors which exerts consistent, responsible attention to every last detail and brings a quiet expertise to matters social, practical and financial, with the ability to work together—against all the prognostications of the men whose wives founded the Colony. This is remarkable in the true sense of that word.

To better exercise their assumed task the Governors delegate the work to heads of committees, who seem to be able, at the monthly meetings, to establish the true character of the Club and work imperceptibly to set its unique tone.

Having worked on these committees and many others in the city, I have been truly astounded at the professionalism of the committee heads and

MODERN TIMES

Mrs. John A. Morris (144 years of the "All Scarlett") and Mrs. Thomas Mellon Evans (Buckland Farm) with red roses, presented by Mrs. Stanley F. Reed. They have just given the Club members a memorable evening on "thoroughbred racing." Mrs. Edward T. Chase who masterminded the evening is at the right.

their true and unerring gift of leadership. At the monthly meetings the general atmosphere of attention and easy flow of relationship is quickly established; reports are given precisely and succinctly and difficulties exposed.

Time is never wasted at committee meetings; opinions are stated in well-modulated voices in a very personal vocabulary, yet in objective terms, discussion is lively, yet controlled gracefully and with humor by the chair.

There has been no dissension or tension although matters are often extremely controversial, yet each problem receives consideration as facts are so quickly verified by the amazingly intensive homework of the chairman, who thereby also reveals her considerate interaction with the staff.

The chairman has in a most subtle way drawn each committee member into the concerns of the Club, has democratically allowed for free speech and open opinion, and has left each member of the committee with a feeling of usefulness. Drawing the threads of the discussion together, she ends the meeting.

The above description of an average Colony Club committee meeting sounds like a textbook reading, but it is only a normal day of "business as usual" at the Colony Club.

• • •

After much thought, this history is concluded by quoting one of our earliest members, Mrs. Albert P. Loening. She joined the Colony Club in 1916 and then left for France to drive an ambulance with Miss Anne Morgan. Years later, she returned to school, and was graduated from college in 1983 at eighty-six years of age!

Mrs. Loening has won pistol-shooting contests, many blue ribbons for her champion hunting dogs, and is noted for her Biblical Garden at the Cathedral of St. John the Divine. She has published nine books. Her latest, *Vignettes of a Life*, has a chapter on the Colony Club. Here is how she ends it:

Yes, the Colony Club is unique. It is a friendly, gracious place that has a deep place in my heart—a second home that I truly love.

I smile now when I recall Mother's words, "You will love it."

How right she was. I do love the Colony Club and all it stands for.

APPENDIX

FOUNDING MEMBERS
Organization Committee, December 1903

Mrs. Archibald Alexander
Mrs. Henry Alexander
Mrs. John Jacob Astor
Miss Helen Barney
Mrs. R. Livingston Beeckman
Mrs. Hamilton Bell
Mrs. Reginald Bishop
Miss Kate Brice
Mrs. James A. Burden, Jr.
Mrs. Cass Canfield
Miss Margaret Chanler
Mrs. Henry Clews
Mrs. John E. Cowdin
Mrs. Walter Damrosch
Miss Caroline de Forest
Mrs. S. Barton French
Mrs. J. Borden Harriman
Miss Mary Harriman
Mrs. Thomas Hastings
Mrs. Richard Irvin

Miss Maud Livingston
Miss Elizabeth Marbury
Mrs. James Markoe
Mrs. Walter Maynard
Miss Anne T. Morgan
Miss Ruth Morgan
Miss Ursula Morgan •
Mrs. A. Gordon Norrie
Mrs. H. Fairfield Osborn
Miss Mary Parsons
Mrs. William S. Rainsford
Miss Florence Rhett
Mrs. William G. Rockefeller
Mrs. George Salisbury
Mrs. W.B. Smith
Mrs. Marion Story
Mrs. Robert Sturges
Mrs. Harry P. Whitney
Mrs. Payne Whitney
Mrs. Egerton Winthrop, Jr.

PRESIDENTS

1904–1917	Mrs. J. Borden Harriman
1917–1924	Miss Ruth Morgan
1924–1929	Mrs. Seymour L. Cromwell
1929–1935	Mrs. James A. Burden
1935–1941	Mrs. Montgomery Hare
1941–1946	Mrs. Henry James
1946–1952	Mrs. Langbourne M. Williams, Jr.
1952–1957	Mrs. Reginald P. Rose
1957–1962	Mrs. Gordon S. Rentschler
1962–1966	Mrs. Hermann G. Place
1966–1972	Mrs. Walter S. Gifford
1972–1976	Mrs. Robert James Lewis
1976–1980	Mrs. Charles I. Pierce, Jr.
1980–1984	Mrs. Stanley F. Reed, Jr.
1984–	Mrs. Bradley I. Collins

FIRST VICE-PRESIDENTS

1904–1917	Mrs. Richard Irvin
1917–1924	Miss Mary Parsons
1924–1930	Mrs. James A. Burden
1930–1936	Mrs. Montgomery Hare
1936–1938	Mrs. Linzee Blagden
1938–1944	Mrs. Henry James
1944–1946	Mrs. Frank Lyon Polk
1946–1950	Mrs. Arnold Whitrïdge
1950–1952	Mrs. Morris Hadley
1952–1970	Mrs. John B. Marsh
1970–1972	Mrs. William B. Given, Jr.
1972–1974	Mrs. William Ward Foshay
1974–1976	Mrs. Walter A. Kernan
1976–1980	Mrs. Stanley F. Reed, Jr.
1980–1984	Mrs. Bradley I. Collins
1984–	Mrs. Cochran B. Supplee

HONORARY VICE-PRESIDENT

1944–1948	Mrs. Egerton L. Winthrop, Jr.

SECOND VICE-PRESIDENTS

1904–1910	Mrs. John Jacob Astor
1910–1913	Mrs. Egerton L. Winthrop, Jr.
1913–1914	Miss Mary Parsons
1914–1915	Mrs. Archibald S. Alexander
1915–1916	Mrs. Egerton L. Winthrop, Jr.
1916–1920	Mrs. Frank Gray Griswold
1920–1944	Mrs. Egerton L. Winthrop, Jr.
1944–1946	Mrs. Harrie T. Lindeberg
1946–1950	Mrs. William Jay Schieffelin, Jr.
1950–1952	Mrs. John B. Marsh
1952–1958	Mrs. Roger Cortesi
1958–1962	Mrs. Hermann G. Place
1962–1966	Mrs. Walter S. Gifford
1966–1970	Mrs. William B. Given, Jr.
1970–1972	Mrs. Robert James Lewis
1972–1976	Mrs. Hugh E. Paine
1976–1980	Mrs. Walter A. Kernan
1980–1984	Mrs. Cochran B. Supplee
1984–	Mrs. Walter A. Kernan

SECRETARIES

1904–1909	Mrs. Walter Damrosch
1909–1911	Mrs. Francis Higginson Cabot
1911–1913	Mrs. Arthur Iselin
1913–1916	Miss Ruth V. Twombly
1916–1922	Mrs. Magee Ellsworth
1922–1924	Mrs. Seymour L. Cromwell
1924–1930	Mrs. Courtlandt D. Barnes
1930–1938	Mrs. Hamilton Fish Armstrong
1938–1946	Mrs. William Greenough
1946–1952	Mrs. Charles H. Russell, Jr.
1952–1956	Mrs. Roger Cortesi
1956–1970	Mrs. Byron Stookey
1970–1974	Mrs. Francis H. Low
1974–1976	Mrs. Francis J. Rue, Jr.
1976–1978	Mrs. Allen F. Maulsby
1978–1980	Mrs. A. Stanton Maulsby
1980–1984	Mrs. Herbert W. Warden II
1984–	Mrs. Peter Van Ness Philip

ASSISTANT SECRETARIES

1946–1948	Mrs. William Greenough
1948–1952	Mrs. Roger Cortesi

TREASURERS

1904–1914	Miss Anne Tracy Morgan
1914–1915	Mrs. Payne Whitney
1915–1916	Mrs. Walter E. Maynard
1916–1930	Mrs. Ruth V. Twombly
1930–1936	Mrs. Cass Canfield
1936–1938	Mrs. Wilton Lloyd-Smith
1938–1940	Mrs. Langbourne M. Williams, Jr.
1940–1944	Mrs. John D.W. Churchill
1944–1951	Mrs. Gordon S. Rentschler
1951–1952	Mrs. Thomas W. Streeter (pro tem)
1952–1956	Mrs. Gordon S. Rentschler
1956–1967	Mrs. William B. Given, Jr.
1967–1972	Mrs. E. Wise Mills
1972–1974	Mrs. Walter A. Kernan
1974–1976	Mrs. Stanley F. Reed, Jr.
1976–1980	Mrs. Charles F. Morgan
1980–1982	Mrs. Frank Richards Ford III
1982–1984	Mrs. Mary Hope Lewis
1984–	Mrs. Adams H. Nickerson

HONORARY MEMBERS
1905–1984

1906	Mrs. Charles T. Barney	1956	Mrs. J. Borden Harriman
1907	Mrs. Stanford White	1956	Mrs. August Belmont
1907	Mrs. Pierpont Morgan	1960	Mrs. Charles A. Lindley
1910	Miss Louisa Lee Schuyler	1964	Mrs. Winthrop Ames
1911	Miss Jane Addams	1976	Mrs. Alden S. Blodgett
1954	Mrs. Selden Bacon		(Cornelia Otis Skinner)

ADVISORY BOARD MEMBERS
Advisors, 1905–1984

J. Pierpont Morgan	George Whitney
Charles T. Barney	James H. Townsend
Frank Lyon Polk	Clarence G. Michalis
R.H. Williams	Juan T. Trippe
Thomas W. Lamont	Thomas S. Gates
Sherman Day	Nelson Adams
Robert P. Perkins	Frank S. Streeter
James H. Perkins	Ellmore C. Patterson
S. Sloan Colt	Charles Scribner, Jr.
Leighton Coleman	John R. Stevenson

COLONY CLUB COMMITTEE CHAIRMEN
HOUSE COMMITTEE

1907–1910	Miss Elizabeth Marbury
1910–1912	Miss Mary Parsons
1912–1913	Mrs. Walter E. Maynard
1913–1914	Miss Caroline deForest
1914–1918	Mrs. Stephen H. Olin
1918–1920	Mrs. Francis McNeil Bacon
1920–1922	Mrs. John T. Pratt
1922–1924	Mrs. Morris W. Kellogg
1924–1926	Mrs. S. Breck Parkman Trowbridge
1926–1928	Miss Louise M. Iselin
1928–1938	Mrs. S. Breck Parkman Trowbridge
1938–1946	Mrs. Harry Horton Benkard
1946–1948	Mrs. Franklin Chase Hoyt
1948–1952	Mrs. Reginald P. Rose
1952–1956	Mrs. Arthur W. Butler
1960–1962	Mrs. John D. Beals
1962–1966	Mrs. F. Richards Ford

HOUSE COMMITTEE *(continued)*

1966–1972	Mrs. Hugh E. Paine
1972–1974	Mrs. Louis Reynal
1974–1976	Mrs. Phoebe Rentschler Stanton
1976–1980	Mrs. Bradley I. Collins
1980–1984	Mrs. Peter Van Ness Philip
1984–	Mrs. James Hoban Harris

Subcommittee on Food

1958–1960	Mrs. Henry W. Cave
1960–1962	Mrs. F. Richards Ford
1962–1964	Mrs. Hugh E. Paine
1964–1966	Mrs. Louis Reynal
1966–1970	Mrs. Rowland Stebbins
1970–1972	Mrs. Jose M. Ferrer, Jr.
1972–1976	Mrs. John D. Garrison
1976–1980	Mrs. John S. Tilney
1980–1984	Mrs. Walter J.P. Curley
1984–	Mrs. Robert M. Day

Subcommittee on Cards

1946–1960	Mrs. William Marston Seabury
1960–1966	Mrs. C. Burrows Freeman

(This Subcommittee moved to Committee on Literature and Arts.)

Subcommittee on Decoration

1960–1966	Mrs. John B. Trevor, Jr.
1966–1968	Mrs. Reginald P. Rose
1968–1974	Mrs. William Ward Foshay
1974–1978	Mrs. Peter Van Ness Philip
1978–1982	Mrs. James Hoban Harris
1982–	Mrs. Cruger D.G. Fowler, Jr.

Subcommittee on Flower Arrangements

1957–1958	Mrs. Paul Sturtevant
1958–1960	Mrs. Paul Sturtevant
	Mrs. Herman D. Ruhm, Jr.
1960–1964	Mrs. Herman D. Ruhm, Jr.
1964–1968	Mrs. James L. Harrison
1968–1976	Mrs. Madison Lewis
1976–1980	Mrs. W. Leicester van Leer
1980–1982	Mrs. Jean C.G. Cornet
1982–1984	Mrs. William Everdell
1984–	Mrs. James J. Beha

Subcommittee Christmas Decorations

1968–1970   Mrs. Herman D. Ruhm, Jr.
1970–1978   Mrs. Malcolm Smith
             Mrs. Frederic P. Houston
1978–   Mrs. Frederic P. Houston

Subcommittee Blue Book

1983–   Mrs. Alfred L. Malabre, Jr.

Subcommittee on Welfare

1915   Miss Harriette Rogers
1916   Mrs. J. Frederic Tams
1917   Miss Harriette Rogers

FINANCE COMMITTEE

1909–1912   Mrs. Heber Reginald Bishop
1912–1914   Mrs. Frank Gray Griswold

AUDITING AND FINANCE COMMITTEE

1914–1924   Mrs. Frank Gray Griswold
1924–1926   Mrs. Winthrop W. Aldrich
1926–1928   Mrs. John T. Pratt
1928–1940   Mrs. Morris W. Kellogg
1940–1942   Miss Ruth V. Twombly
1942–1944   Mrs. Langbourne M. Williams, Jr.
1944–1948   Mrs. Morris Hadley
1948–1952   Mrs. Robert H. Thayer
1952–1958   Mrs. Thomas W. Streeter

FINANCE COMMITTEE

1958–1966   Mrs. Walter S. Gifford
1966–1971   Mrs. William B. Given, Jr.
1971–1972   Mrs. Walter B. Devereux
1972–1974   Mrs. John Elliott, Jr.
1974–1976   Mrs. Walter A. Kernan
1976–1980   Mrs. Ellmore C. Patterson
1980–1984   Mrs. Adams H. Nickerson
1984–   Mrs. Harry W. Fowler

COMMITTEE ON LITERATURE AND ARTS

1909	Mrs. Walter E. Maynard
1910–1913	Mrs. Payne Whitney
1913–1914	Miss Beatrice Bend
1914–1918	Mrs. Seymour L. Cromwell
1918–1926	Mrs. James A. Burden
1926–1933	Mrs. Linzee Blagden
1933–1938	Mrs. W. Murray Crane
1938–1940	Mrs. Harrie T. Lindeberg
1940–1942	Mrs. Charles A. Lindley
1942–1946	Mrs. Jarvis Cromwell
1946–1948	Mrs. Frank Parsons Shepard
1948–1950	Mrs. D. Percy Morgan
1950–1954	Mrs. George L. Harrison
1954–1956	Mrs. Frank Parsons Shepard
1956–1960	Mrs. Hermann G. Place
1960–1962	Mrs. Clarence G. Michalis
1962–1964	Mrs. Donald M. Oenslager
1964–1976	Mrs. Robert de Vecchi
1976–1984	Mrs. Edward T. Chase
1984–	Mrs. Daniel P. Davison

Subcommittee on Cards
(moved from House Committee)

1966–1970	Mrs. Ryder Henry
1970–1974	Mrs. Charles S. Whitman, Jr.
1974–1978	Mrs. Theodore F. Whitmarsh
1978–1980	Mrs. James J. Beha
1980–	Mrs. Alexander O. Vietor

Subcommittee on Entertainment

1958–1962	Mrs. John Kean
1962–1966	Mrs. John A. Morris
1966–1976	Mrs. Rushmore Patterson
1976–1978	Mrs. Frank Richards Ford III
1978–1984	Mrs. John A. Hardy, Jr.
1984–	Mrs. Haebler Frantz

Subcommittee on Exhibitions

1915–1917	Mrs. Payne Whitney
1917–1919	Mrs. Allen Tucker
1919–1922	Mrs. Harry Payne Whitney
1922–1924	Mrs. Meredith Hare
1924–1944	Mrs. Egerton L. Winthrop, Jr.

Subcommittee on Library

1915–1916	Mrs. Archer M. Huntington
1916–1917	Mrs. George C. Riggs
1917–1918	Mrs. Victor Morawetz
1918–1922	Miss C. L. Frelinghuysen
1922–1924	Mrs. F. Louis Slade
1924–1926	Mrs. Stephen H. Olin
1926–1952	Mrs. Austin Strong
1952–1971	Mrs. Sherman Post Haight
1971–1972	Mrs. Sherman Post Haight
	Miss Julia P. Wightman
1972–1973	Miss Julia P. Wightman
1973–1974	Mrs. Hugh Bullock
1974–1980	Mrs. Harold H. Healy, Jr.
1980–1984	Mrs. Charles F. Morgan
1984–	Mrs. Howard E. Cox

Subcommitte on Programs

1915–1924	Mrs. Gordon Norrie
1924–1926	Mrs. Linzee Blagden
1926–1928	Mrs. Walter E. Maynard
1928–1930	Mrs. Pleasants Pennington
1930–1940	Mrs. Winthrop Ames
1940–1942	Mrs. Elbridge Gerry Chadwick
1942–1944	Miss Fanny M. Cottenet

COMMITTEE ON BATHS AND ATHLETICS

1909–1912	Miss Florence M. Rhett
1912–1916	Mrs. Francis Higginson Cabot
1916–1917	Mrs. W. Bourke Cockran
1917–1918	Mrs. James Stewart Cushman
1918–1920	Mrs. Grafton Howland Pyne
1920–1922	Mrs. Morris W. Kellogg
1922–1924	Mrs. J. Peter Hoguet
1924–1926	Mrs. John T. Pratt
1926–1928	Mrs. Winthrop W. Aldrich
1928–1930	Mrs. Francis Higginson Cabot
1930–1936	Mrs. Richard F. Babcock
1936–1938	Mrs. James Watson Webb
1938–1940	Mrs. Frank Lyon Polk

1940–1946	Mrs. Pratt McLane
1946–1948	Mrs. Alexander P. Morgan
1948–1956	Mrs. Samuel W. Lambert, Jr.
1956–1960	Mrs. Chauncey Belknap
1960–1964	Mrs. R. Townley Paton
1964–1966	Mrs. L. Lee Stanton
1966–1970	Mrs. Eduardo Andrade
1970–1974	Mrs. John B. Aspegren
1974–1978	Mrs. L. Robertson Hatch
1978–1980	Mrs. Cochran B. Supplee
1980–1982	Mrs. Grover O'Neill, Jr.
1982–	Mrs. Kathryn D. O'Neill

Subcommittee on Sports

1915–1916	Miss Maude K. Wetmore
1916–1917	Mrs. Lewis Gouverneur Morris

Subcommittee on Baths

1938–1940	Mrs. J.C. Rathborne
1940–1942	Mrs. Harrie T. Lindeberg
1942–1946	Mrs. Francis C. Bishop
1946	Mrs. W. Allston Flagg

Subcommittee on Hairdressing

1938–1940	Mrs. B. Brewster Jennings
1940–1942	Mrs. Donald P. Blagden
1942–1946	Mrs. Frederic W. Lincoln

Subcommittee on Gymnasium

1938–1940	Mrs. Pratt McLane

Subcommittee on Boutique

1980–	Mrs. Michael N. Ambler

COMMITTEE ON MEMBERSHIP

1948–1950	Mrs. Charles H. Russell, Jr.
1950–1954	Mrs. Roger Cortesi
1954–1970	Mrs. Byron Stookey
1970–1976	Mrs. Charles I. Pierce, Jr.
1976–1980	Mrs. W. Rice Brewster
1980–1982	Mrs. Walter A. Kernan
1982–	Mrs. John Wilson Espy

Subcommittee for Honorary Visitors

1976–   Mrs. Hugh Bullock

YOUNGER MEMBERS COMMITTEE

1963–1964	Mrs. Harold H. Healy, Jr.
1964–1966	Mrs. Richard Kimball
	Mrs. Frank S. Streeter
1966–1967	Mrs. Harry W. Havemeyer
	Mrs. Henry L. King
1967–1968	Mrs. Harry W. Havemeyer
	Mrs. Theron O. Worth, Jr.
1968–1970	Mrs. Theron O. Worth, Jr.
	Mrs. Michael N. Ambler
1970–1972	Mrs. Michael N. Ambler
1972–1974	Mrs. John Wilson Espy
1974–1976	Mrs. Hamilton Southworth, Jr.
1976–1978	Mrs. George Crawford, Jr.
1978–1980	Mrs. Eustace de Cordova, Jr.
1980–1982	Mrs. Harald S. deRopp
1982–1984	Miss Charlotte McKim
1984–	Mrs. Robert W. Sheehan

BUILDING COMMITTEE

1915–1916   Miss Mary Parsons

SPECIAL COMMITTEE WAR RELIEF

1942–1946   Mrs. William Jay Schieffelin, Jr.

UNITED NATIONS COMMITTEE

1948   Mrs. Robert H. Thayer

ARCHIVIST

1962–1971	Mrs. Harrie T. Lindeberg
1971–	Mrs. John B. Marsh

In 1905, before there was a clubhouse, the first yearbook listed the following Governors:

Mrs. Archibald S. Alexander
Mrs. John Jacob Astor
Mrs. Reginald Bishop
Miss Kate Brice
Mrs. John E. Cowdin
Mrs. Walter Damrosch
Miss Caroline de Forest

Mrs. J. Borden Harriman
Miss Mary Harriman
Mrs. Thomas Hastings
Mrs. Richard Irvin
Miss Elizabeth Marbury
Mrs. Walter Maynard
Miss Anne Morgan

Mrs. Henry F. Osborn
Miss Mary Parsons
Mrs. W. S. Rainsford
Miss Florence Rhett
Mrs. Egerton L.
   Winthrop, Jr.
Mrs. Payne Whitney

Others who have served as Governors through the years are the following:

Mrs. Charles B. Alexander
Mrs. Vincent Astor
Mrs. Winthrop W. Aldrich
Mrs. Hamilton Fish
   Armstrong
Mrs. Winthrop Ames
Mrs. Eduardo Andrade
Mrs. John Aspegren
Miss Beatrice Bend
Mrs. Francis McNiel
   Bacon, Jr.
Mrs. Robert Bacon
Mrs. August Belmont
Mrs. Courtlandt D. Barnes
Mrs. James A. Burden
Mrs. Linzee Blagden
Mrs. Heber Reginald Bishop
Mrs. Henry W. Bull
Mrs. Richard F. Babcock
Mrs. Harry Horton Benkard
Mrs. Arthur W. Butler
Mrs. Chauncey Belknap
Mrs. Henry C. Breck
Mrs. John D. Beals
Mrs. Hugh Bullock
Mrs. W. Rice Brewster
Mrs. Francis Higginson
   Cabot
Mrs. Seymour L. Cromwell
Mrs. James Stewart Cushman
Mrs. W. Bourke Cockran
Miss Mabel Choate
Mrs. Guy Fairfax Cary

Mrs. Cass Canfield
Mrs. W. Murray Crane
Mrs. John D. W. Churchill
Mrs. Jarvis Cromwell
Mrs. Roger Cortesi
Mrs. Henry W. Cave
Mrs. Bradley I. Collins
Mrs. Edward T. Chase
Mrs. Daniel G. Collins
Mrs. Walter J. P. Curley
Mrs. Marshall J. Dodge
Mrs. Joseph E. Davis
Mrs. Robert de Vecchi
Mrs. Walter B. Devereux
Mrs. Daniel P. Davison
Mrs. Magee Ellsworth
Mrs. Daniel W. Evans
Mrs. Frederick M. Eaton
Mrs. John Elliott, Jr.
Mrs. William Everdell III
Mrs. John Wilson Espy
Mrs. Charles Fairchild
   Fuller
Mrs. Edwin A. Fish
Mrs. W. Allston Flagg
Mrs. William Ward Foshay
Mrs. H. Bartow Farr
Mrs. F. Richards Ford
Mrs. C. Burrows Freeman
Mrs. Harry W. Fowler
Mrs. George A. Fowlkes
Mrs. Fergus Reid, Jr.
Mrs. Frank Gray Griswold

Mrs. William Greenough
Mrs. William B. Given
Mrs. Walter S. Gifford
Mrs. J. Peter Hoguet
Mrs. Montgomery Hare
Mrs. Charles F. Havemeyer
Mrs. Morris Hadley
Mrs. E. Roland Harriman
Mrs. Franklin C. Hoyt
Mrs. Hamilton Hadden
Mrs. George L. Harrison
Mrs. F.G. Hoppin
Mrs. James L. Harrison
Mrs. L. Robertson Hatch
Mrs. John Fraser Horn
Mrs. James Hoban Harris
Mrs. Arthur Iselin
Miss Louise M. Iselin
Mrs. Oliver Burr James
Mrs. Henry James
Mrs. Morris W. Kellogg
Mrs. G. Hermann
   Kinnicutt
Mrs. Walter A. Kernan
Mrs. Albert L. Key
Mrs. Harrie T. Lindeberg
Mrs. Charles A. Lindley
Mrs. Francis H. Low
Mrs. James F. Lawrence
Mrs. Samuel W.
   Lambert, Jr.
Mrs. Mary Hope Lewis
Miss Ruth Morgan